Francis Hopkinson Smith

Well-worn roads in Spain, Holland, and Italy

Francis Hopkinson Smith

Well-worn roads in Spain, Holland, and Italy

ISBN/EAN: 9783743373044

Manufactured in Europe, USA, Canada, Australia, Japa

Cover: Foto ©Andreas Hilbeck / pixelio.de

Manufactured and distributed by brebook publishing software (www.brebook.com)

Francis Hopkinson Smith

Well-worn roads in Spain, Holland, and Italy

By F. Hopkinson Smith.

OLD LINES IN NEW BLACK AND WHITE. From Lowell, Holmes, and Whittier. With 12 full-page illustrations, from designs in charcoal by F. HOPKINSON SMITH. Oblong folio or in portfolio, $12.00.

THE SAME. *Large-Paper Edition.* With Illustrations printed on Japanese paper, mounted on plate paper. Edition limited to 100 copies. In portfolio (16 x 22 inches), $25.00.

WELL-WORN ROADS OF SPAIN, HOLLAND, AND ITALY, travelled by a Painter in search of the Picturesque. With 16 full-page phototype reproductions of water-color drawings, and text by F. HOPKINSON SMITH, profusely illustrated with pen-and-ink sketches. A Holiday volume. Folio, full gilt, $15.00.

THE SAME. *Popular Edition.* Including some of the illustrations of the above. 16mo, gilt top, $1.25.

A BOOK OF THE TILE CLUB. Containing 114 reproductions of representative Paintings, Bas-Reliefs, Portraits, and Sketches by members of the Tile Club of New York, including 27 full-page phototypes. With Sketch of the Club, and account of one of its Meetings by F. HOPKINSON SMITH and EDWARD STRAHAN. A Holiday volume. Folio, gilt top, $25.00.

THE SAME. *Edition de Luxe.* Limited to 100 copies. With full-page illustrations on Japanese paper. Superbly bound in vellum. Folio, full gilt, $50.00.

A WHITE UMBRELLA IN MEXICO.

HOUGHTON, MIFFLIN & CO.
BOSTON AND NEW YORK.

WELL-WORN ROADS
OF
SPAIN, HOLLAND, AND ITALY

*TRAVELED BY A PAINTER IN SEARCH
OF THE PICTURESQUE*

BY

F. HOPKINSON SMITH

BOSTON AND NEW YORK
HOUGHTON, MIFFLIN AND COMPANY
The Riverside Press, Cambridge
1890

Copyright, 1886 and 1887,
By F. HOPKINSON SMITH.

All rights reserved.

The Riverside Press, Cambridge, Mass., U. S. A.
Electrotyped and Printed by H. O. Houghton & Company.

𝔍𝔫 𝔑𝔢𝔪𝔢𝔪𝔟𝔯𝔞𝔫𝔠𝔢 of the many happy days we have spent together, tramping and sketching, along roads well worn and loved, and as a slight personal tribute to his genius, I dedicate this book to the memory of my friend,

ARTHUR QUARTLEY,

an open-hearted man, an out-door painter of the highest rank, and a loyal lover of Nature.

F. HOPKINSON SMITH.

NEW YORK, *September 10, 1886.*

CONTENTS

	PAGE
INTRODUCTION	1
THE CHURCH OF SAN PABLO, SEVILLE	4
EL PUERTA DEL VINO. ALHAMBRA (GRANADA)	9
A GYPSY DANCE NEAR GRANADA	15
UNDER ARREST IN CORDOVA	28
A VERANDA IN THE ALCAZARIA	38
IN AND OUT OF A CAB IN AMSTERDAM	46
A WATER-LOGGED TOWN IN HOLLAND	58
Under a Balcony	62
A Day with the Professor	66
A Visit from the Doctor	71
ON THE RIVA, VENICE	77
A SUMMER'S DAY IN VENICE	87
THE TOP OF A GONDOLA	96
BEHIND THE RIALTO	106
UP A BELFRY IN BAVARIA	113

INTRODUCTION

THESE sketches are the record of some idle days spent in rambling about odd places, and into quaint nooks, and along well-worn roads of travel. They contain no information of any value to anybody. They are absolutely bare of statistics, are entirely useless as a guide to travelers, and can be of no possible benefit to a student desirous of increasing his knowledge either of foreign architecture, mediæval art, politics, or any kindred subject.

They are not arranged in any order, have no specific bearing one upon the other, and are, in short, the merest outline of what one may see and hear who keeps both his eyes and his ears wide open.

They were written some months after the discomforts and annoyances of travel had passed out of mind, and when only the memory remained of the many happy hours spent under cool archways, and along canals, and up curious, twisted streets, and into dark, old, smoked churches. They, however, possess one quality, and that is truth.

A painter has peculiar advantages over other less fortunate people. His sketch-book is a passport and his white umbrella a flag of truce in all lands under the sun, be it savage or civilized; an "open sesame," bringing good cheer and hospitality, and entitling the possessor to all the benefits of liberty, equality, and fraternity.

I have been picked up on a roadside in Cuba by a Spanish grandee, who has driven me home in his volante to breakfast. I have been left in charge of the priceless relics and treasures of old Spanish churches hours at a time and alone. I have had my beer mug filled to the brim by mountaineers in the Tyrolean Alps, and had a chair placed for me at the table of a Dutchman living near the Zuider Zee. All these courtesies and civilities being the result of only ten minutes' previous acquaintance, and simply because I was a painter.

Truly "one touch of nature [with the brush] makes the whole world kin."

If, therefore, by reason of my craft and its advantages, I can show you some things you may perhaps have overlooked in your own wanderings, I shall be more than satisfied. So if you will draw another easy chair up to my studio fire I will tell you as simply as I can something of the groups who looked over my shoulder while I worked, and who daily formed my circle of acquaintance ; merely hinting to you as delicately as possible that a traveler, even with an ordinary pair of eyes and ears, can get much nearer to the heart of a people in their cafés, streets, and markets than in their museums, galleries, and palaces, and reminding you at the same time of the old adage which claims that "a live gamin is better than a dead king," for all the practical purposes of life.

F. H. S.

NEW YORK, *September*, 1886.

THE CHURCH OF SAN PABLO, SEVILLE

I HAD a queer adventure in this old Spanish church. I was a voluntary prisoner within its quiet walls for half a day. The intense heat of the morning had driven me out of the small plaza near the fruit market, and into a narrow, crooked street which led to the open church door. The interior was filled with the fragrant incense of the mass, just closed, and the cool air and silence of the place were so grateful that I laid my "trap" softly down near a group of pillars, uncovered my head, and watched the kneeling figures praying at the feet of the Virgin. Two altar boys entered from a side door, snuffed out the long candles, and covered the altar with white cloths. One by one the kneeling penitents rose, bowed reverently, drew their mantillas closer, and glided out into the sunlight. Soon the sacristan appeared, closed the great swinging-doors behind the last worshiper, and discovered me with my easel up. I had already blocked in one end of the confessional, over which hung poised in air a huge angel, holding a swinging-lamp.

"Señor, it is not permitted to remain longer. It is eleven o'clock. At four you can return again."

Two pesetas performed a miracle. The sacristan was soon in the hot street with the money and the keys in his pocket, and I was locked up alone in the cool church with my easel and sketch. I continued painting. The hours wore on slowly. The light streamed in through the high windows, patterned the floor, crept up the altar steps, and illumined the head of the huge angel with a crown of prismatic color.

The silence became intense, and was broken only by the muffled sound of a door closing in the cloister beyond. Suddenly a panel opened in the solid wall to my left, and a figure closely veiled and shrouded in black tottered in, supported by her duenna and an elderly woman. She staggered to the altar steps, and threw back her mantilla. She was richly dressed, deathly pale, and her eyes red with weeping. With a cry of agony she lifted up her hands, and fell half swooning at the feet of the figure of the Virgin.

"Mi adorada amiga!" she sobbed, "they have taken you away. Mother of God, have mercy!" The duenna raised her head and laid it in her lap. The mother sat silently by, smoothing her temples and fanning softly. Again she raised herself, and, winding her white arms around the Virgin, while her black hair streamed over her tear-stained face, she poured out her grief, until she sank back exhausted and motionless. This continued nearly an hour, — the señorita sobbing convulsively, and the two women kneeling beside her, waiting for the paroxysms to pass, until, utterly worn out, she was lifted and half carried across the aisle and through the open door. It closed gently and left no trace.

I emerged from my shelter, gathered up my brushes, and continued work. The confessional box took definite shape, and the angel was kept in his proper place by many pats of color bestowed on the back-

ground around him. A few touches
brought out the swinging-lamp and the organ-pipes against the light high up in the
nave. But I could not paint. I pushed
back my easel and began wandering about.
I sat down by the altar steps, near where
the señorita had thrown herself, and examined carefully the poor cracked image
of the Virgin, with the paint scaling off
and crumbling under my touch, to which
she had clung so desperately. I went on
tiptoe to the altar. The old Spanish chairs
on either side were covered with soiled
linen covers; underneath, huge brass nails
of a Moorish pattern, and scarlet velvet,
threadbare. The vessels, quaint in design,
silvered on copper. The cloths, superb
with delicate Salamanca embroidery in pale
yellow and white. The lamp which hung
in front, suspended from a chain lost in the
gloom of the roof, burned a ruby light.
Behind the altar, broken saints of wood and
plaster, bits of candles, tapers, and the
ashes of many censers. Behind this, a circular stairway leading to the organ loft.
Up this stairway, dust, and a lumber-room
containing old chant-books bound in vellum, yellow and worm-eaten, with bronze

corners and heavy bindings torn and defaced. Farther on, a small door, and then the organ. The floor was strewn with broken keys, twisted pipes and wire, and the great tubes were smashed in as if with the butt of a musket. I again closed the small door, and descended the stairway. A key grated in a lock, the great door swung open, and let in the sunlight, the hot air, and the sacristan.

Had I been disturbed? Yes, the señorita. He looked startled.

Through which door? Ah! yes; from the Archbishop's. He had heard about it. It was very sad. The poor señorita, and she so beautiful!

"But is there no hope?"

"No, mi amigo; he was shot at daylight."

EL PUERTA DEL VINO. ALHAMBRA (GRANADA)

THE legends say that the Moorish kings stored their choicest wine in the cellars beneath this curious old archway. It was blazing away this morning at a white heat under a Spanish sun and against a china-blue sky, and it sheltered not the juice of the grape, but an aguador and two donkeys. All three were asleep, — the water-carrier on his back, and the patient, tired little beasts propped up against each other.

They had climbed the long hill of the Alhambra very many times since sunrise, and the water-jars had been often filled that day, and as often emptied into thirsty villagers in the plain below. They had refreshed everybody but themselves. Now it was their turn. So they dozed away, and I continued painting.

If their green jars had contained wine I should have had no use for it. No water-color painter does. But water, pure water, began to be valuable; my bottle was empty, and the well some distance off. It was cruel to disturb them, but after all I am only human. "Agua? Si, señor." The aguador sprang to his feet, the donkeys lazily opened their eyes, a simultaneous convulsive movement of long ears and short tails, and the procession moved down out into the glare, and halted outside of my umbrella.

A glass wet and held high, glistening in the sunlight, a shower of diamond drops thrown in a circle, a gurgling sound from a cool jar, and, with the bow of an Hidalgo, the aguador handed me that most blessed of all drinks, — cool water in a hot land. I dropped a copper into his outstretched hand, and looked up. He was a tall, straight young fellow, swarthy, with high cheek-bones, and black, bead-like eyes; a red silk handkerchief bound his head, and a broad sash encircled his waist.

"You are not a Spaniard?" I asked.

His face flushed, and a smile of supreme contempt crept over it.

"A Spaniard? Caramba! No, señor! I am a gypsy! Come."

He caught me by the arm, and half dragged me to the low wall which overhangs the plain. Below was the valley of the Vega and the city of Granada swimming in a gray dust. He pointed to a narrow road far down the slope, skirted by the river Darro.

"See you those dark holes in the hillside? That is my home." I made him a low bow. I had not only caught a gypsy, but a cave-dweller.

I remembered instantly that this man's ancestors lived in these holes in the ground before Ibn-I-Ahmar began to build the Alhambra. I also remembered that the Moors had "met with some reverses;" but here was this sunburnt gypsy living in a house eight hundred years old, and the house still in possession of his family! I handed him a cigarette, and made room for him under my umbrella.

His story was very simple. He had been a water-carrier for several years. In the summer time he earned two pesetas (about forty cents). The donkeys belonged to his father, who had half of his earnings. That left one peseta for himself and Pepita.

Was Pepita his wife? No, not yet, because her mother had been a long time sick; but soon — perhaps by next Holy Week.

He wished I knew Pepita. "Her waist was so" (making a circle of his two thumbs and his two forefingers), "her ankle was so" (one thumb and one forefinger), "and her foot so" (holding up his little finger).

Pepita was as good as she was pretty. Perhaps she would come up to the well to-day, for she was at mass when he left that morning. He would go to the well and look for her.

He was gone a long time, and but for the dozing donkeys broiling in the sun I should have given him up.

Suddenly four long ears pointed forward, and two stumpy tails veered like weather-vanes. Through the archway came my aguador and the daintiest of little gypsy maidens. She wore a white kerchief tied under her chin, great hoops of gold in her ears, strings of blue beads around her neck and wrists, over her shoulders a yellow scarf, and on her feet tiny black slippers with red heels. Shading her eyes with her fan she gave me a timid courtesy, and stood at one side, resting her hand on her lover's shoulder. She watched every movement of my brush, and laughed heartily when a few strokes indicated the donkeys.

But it was growing late. Would the most illustrious painter have any more water? Would he share the grapes Pepita had brought? Yes, with pleasure; but Pepita should have five pesetas.

Shall I tell you what happened as I placed the coins in her hands?

"Ah, señor! Bueno! bueno! Mateo, see!" she said, holding up the money and seizing my hand, her eyes filling with tears. Before I was aware she had kissed it.

The aguador leaned forward and whispered, "You know her mother is very sick."

Then he fumbled about between the donkeys, and piled both panniers and all the jars on top of the uglier and sleepier of the two, and the dainty little sweetheart was lifted on the other. Then I watched them through the archway and down the steep hill, until they were lost amid the pomegranates.

I held up the back of my hand. Yes, there was no mistake; she had kissed it. It was a pity that she — but then, of course, I was only a stray painter. I was not an aguador, descendant of a family eight hundred years old, a landed proprietor, with a cash capital of five pesetas, and a half interest in a water-route and two donkeys!

After all, are the good things of this world so unequally divided?

Quien sabe?

A GYPSY DANCE NEAR GRANADA

MATEO, the aguador, and I became great friends. His cheery, bright face, and his welcome "Buenos dias, señor," were very grateful to me so many miles away from home. He and the donkeys stumbled in upon me at all hours, and in all parts of the Alhambra grounds; and if he did not quickly catch sight of my white umbrella, he would leave his little beasts in the road and go in search of me.

This afternoon I heard his voice far down the hill, and in a few moments more he came singing through the small entrance gate, and, bursting into a laugh, began to tell me the latest news in the city below.

He was especially delighted over the padre who sold the chairs out of the sacristy to the Englishman, and who did not give all the money to the bishop. This I knew to be true, for I had a hand in a similar transaction myself, — the chair I write in being part of the villainy.

He had a sad story to tell about Santiago, who lived at the Great Gate, and whose brother, the matador, had been hurt in the bull-fight.

Then he told me about the actor from Madrid, who lived in one of the old red towers of the Alhambra, and who came every summer with a new wife; about the mass on Sunday last, the procession of Holy Week; and the great Spaniard who lived in Paris, and who visited his olive farm only once in five years, and who arrived yesterday. Then, finally, about Pepita. I began to notice that all these talks ended in Pepita. To-day he was in fine spirits. He had already earned three pesetas, and it was not yet sundown.

It was a "Fiesta day," and the churches and streets were full, and the people very thirsty. To-night he and Pepita would go to the dance.

Up to this time I listened to his talk without ever looking up from my work. I was struggling with the Moorish arch over the entrance of the Hall of the Ambassadors, and had my hands full, but here I laid down my palette.

"What dance, Mateo?"

"The dance of the gypsies, señor, at the Posada del Albaycin. La Tonta would dance, and the king of the gypsies would bring his great guitar. Would the illustrious painter accompany them?"

That being the one particular thing the illustrious painter most desired to see in all Granada, I at once accepted, hurried up my work, and arranged to meet them at the Great Gate of Charles V. Accordingly about an hour after sundown I gave my watch and wallet to the landlord, took my umbrella-staff, and strolled down the hill.

Mateo awaited me in the shadow of the arch of the gate, carrying a lantern. Pepita joined us farther down in the city; she had stopped on her way up to restring her guitar. In a few moments more we all halted at the door of a wine shop in the rear of the church. This was the Posada del Albaycin. A dim lamp fastened against the wall revealed a crowd of aguadores, fruit-sellers, and garlic-venders, together with a motley crew of Spaniards and gypsies of both sexes crowding about the entrance.

As I passed in, I heard overhead the click of the castanets and the low thrumming of the guitars. Ascending the steps, I found myself in a long room on the second floor, simply furnished with a row of chairs on either side, and lighted by a number of lamps suspended on brackets fastened to the wall. At one end was a raised platform covered with a carpet. Seated upon this platform was a man of middle age, very tall and broadly built, with the features and expression of an American Indian. Compared in size to the gypsies about him, he was a giant. He was tuning an enormous guitar,—a very grandfather of guitars—having all the strings which ordinary instruments of its class possess, and an extra string fastened on an outrigger. The back of this curious instrument was covered with sheet-brass.

As we entered he left his chair, placed the guitar against the wall, greeted Mateo and Pepita, and, having spoken in an undertone to the aguador, raised his wide Spanish hat and saluted me gracefully.

Pepita occupied one of the vacant seats on the platform, and rested her instrument gently against her knee, while her lover and I watched the groups as they crowded up the narrow stairway and filled the floor space.

He pointed out all the celebrities. The tall man with the overgrown guitar was known as the king of the gypsies. The dance to-night was for his benefit. La Tonta was his daughter, and the best dancer in Spain. She did not dance often. He was sure I would not be disappointed. But the dance was about to begin, and we must keep silence.

The king bowed to the audience, struck his guitar with the flat of his hand, swept all the strings simultaneously, twirled it in the air, kissed it, took his seat with a great flourish, and began the melody. Immediately, at the far end of the room, a young gypsy arose, tightened his belt, clapped his hands, and began a slow movement with his feet, the dancers and audience keeping time with their castanets and the palms of their hands.

Then a gypsy girl took the floor and danced a "Bolero." Then came more gypsies in tight trousers and loose jackets, until the hour arrived for the sensation of the evening.

A great clapping announced La Tonta as she entered quickly from a side door, and stood facing the mirror. To my surprise she was a tall, thin, ungraceful, badly-formed, and slattern-looking gypsy woman, by no means young. She was attired in a long yellow calico gown hanging loosely about her, much the worse for wear and not overclean. She wore black kid slippers and white cotton stockings. Her skin was dark like all women of her race, and her eyes large and luminous. Her mass of jet-black hair was caught in a twist behind, the whole decorated with blossoms of the tuberose. Taken as a whole, she was the last woman in all Spain you would have picked out as a star danseuse.

I looked at Mateo in surprise, but his expression was too earnest and his admiration too sincere. He evidently did not agree with me in my estimate of La Tonta. He laid his hand upon my knee, and said, "Wait!"

At this instant a stout gypsy in his shirt sleeves, who had been beating time with his cane, and who appeared to be master of ceremonies, cleared the floor, pressing everybody back against the wall.

La Tonta stood surveying herself in the mirror which hung over the mantel. She nodded to Mateo, and began rolling up her soiled calico sleeves quite to her shoulders, revealing a thin, although well-proportioned and not altogether unattractive pair of arms. She then stripped the cheap tinsel bracelets from her wrists, and hid them in her bosom.

As the music increased in volume, she shut her eyes and stretched out her long arms as a panther sometimes does; then lifted them above her head, and instantly they fell into the rhythm of the music. Her feet now began to move, and a peculiar swaying motion started as if from her heels, ran up through her limbs, back, and neck, undulated through her long arms, and lost itself in her finger-tips.

This was repeated again and again, each movement increasing in intensity; her eyes flashing with a light rare even in a Spanish gypsy. She stamped her feet, swayed her body backward and forward, almost touched the floor with her hair, and then suddenly rushed forward, appealing to you with her outstretched arms.

The music seemed to possess her like a spell. She became grace itself, her movements sylph-like — and, if you will believe it, positively beautiful. As the music quickened, her gestures became more violent; as it died away, you could hardly believe she moved — and she did not, except the slight shuffling of her feet, which kept up the spell within her.

The effect on the audience was startling. Men rose to their feet, bending forward and watching her every motion. The women clapped their hands, encouraging her with cries of "Ollé! ollé! Bravo, La Tonta!"

Suddenly the music ceased, and La Tonta stood perfectly still. Her eyes opened, her arms fell limp beside her, her back straightened, and she awoke as if from a trance. Giving a quick glance around, she gathered her skirts in her hand, and limped rather than walked through the hall and out into the side room, if anything more awkward than when she had entered.

The applause was long-continued and genuine. I certainly did my share of it. The look of supreme satisfaction which came over the face of my aguador as he watched my admiration was not the least part of my enjoyment.

But the dance was over, and we all crowded to the street. Mateo had greetings for his friends, and Pepita was surrounded by half a dozen girls of her own age, who had kind things to say about her part of the performance. In a moment I was singled out and besieged by a bevy of dark-eyed gypsies, who had heard, no doubt, of Pepita's good fortune, and who, if they did not have sick mothers at home, had many other interests which were equally pressing.

"Una peseta, señor," called out half a dozen at once. I had a few small coins left in my sketching-coat, but they were soon distributed. "Por me, señor," said a wicked-looking gypsy girl. My money being all gone, and the bulk of my property being at that moment in the hands of my landlord, I did the next best thing possible. I gave her a red rose from my buttonhole with my best bow. Just here my trouble began. She received it with a cold smile, and turned on her heel. In less time thereafter than I can tell it, a young fellow broke through the group and confronted me, held the rose in his hand, poured out a torrent of abuse, and ground it into the earth with his heel.

Mateo sprang forward and caught him by the throat, and for a moment it looked as if there was going to be as lively a scene as I had ever experienced. But at this instant the powerful form of the king appeared in the doorway, and, after mutual explanations on all sides, the young fellow seemed satisfied that no indignity had been offered his sweetheart, and that the illustrious painter had only intended a compliment especially prized by the señoritas in his own country.

With this we separated, Mateo and Pepita going with me as far as the Great Gate, the groups scattering down the crooked streets, and I to wander about the groves of the Alhambra before going to bed.

It was a lovely night, and I wanted once more to see the Garden of Lindaraja with its deep shadows. A few quick steps brought me beyond the archway of the

Gate of Justice, and near the fountains of the Court of Lions.

It was nearly midnight. The Moorish arches, supported on their slender marble columns, wore the color of a tea-rose, as they stood bathed in the moonlight. There was no sound but the gurgling of the water running through the channels in the marble at my feet, and the regular plash of the fountain.

I began thinking about these gypsies — their history, the peculiarities of their race, the stories of their villainy and treachery, of their vindictiveness, of their curious homes, and then of this girl whom the music had transformed into a goddess.

My reverie was broken by the sound of a footstep, and rising from my seat I looked behind me into the mass of shadow. It ceased, and I again took my seat. Some visitor, I thought, who would also see the Alhambra by moonlight. But I felt uncomfortable. The incident of the rose was, to say the least, unpleasant. I began realizing the lateness of the hour, and turned my steps back to my lodgings.

On the way home, finding the bucket of the well of the Moors at the top and full, I had a cool drink. Then I passed down through the trees and into the narrow ravine which leads through the gate, and so on under the archway and out into the moonlight beyond its black shadow.

At that instant I became conscious that some one was following me. I could hear the rapid footfall timed to keep pace with my own. I grasped my umbrella-staff, and slid it along my hand until I could feel the iron spike. As I reached the last outer step of the gate, a man wearing a gypsy's cloak ran rapidly through the shadow behind and toward me. I turned quickly, and recognized the young gypsy who had so pointedly destroyed my rose under his boot heel.

At the same instant another figure glided from the doorway to my side, and said in a low voice, "Never fear, caballero; it is Mateo. I am watching the cut-throat."

The gypsy started back, sprang over the low wall, and disappeared in the darkness. If I had ever been glad to see Mateo it was at that moment. He was out of breath — and temper. For an instant he was undecided whether he would go home with me or go after the gentleman with the destructive heel. I finally persuaded him that he possibly might do both, but he should leave me at my lodgings first.

On our way down the hill Mateo told me his end of the story. After leaving Pepita for the night, and crossing the street which leads to the Great Gate, he had noticed this fellow skulking along, and watched him turn into the Alhambra grounds. Knowing that the gypsy could not reach his home by that route, and remembering our recent difficulty, he had dogged his footsteps into and through the Alhambra, and had caught up with him as I was drinking at the well. Believing that I would go out by the Gate of Justice, he had taken the short cut down the hill, and waited for me under the archway, and I knew the rest.

I reached my lodgings and rapped up the sleepy porter, and bade good-night to my friend the aguador. I hope my additions to Pepita's dowry cured the mother and hastened the wedding.

UNDER ARREST IN CORDOVA

In Spain evolution has produced the tartana from the old-fashioned charcoal cart. During the process the cart lost two of its wheels and the tartana gained two long seats, both chintz covered and made comfortable with pew cushions, besides two pairs of lace curtains looped back fore and aft, and a brief flight of steps farthest from the mule serving as a sort of Jacob's ladder for ascending and descending señoritas.

I was standing in the shadow of one of the gates of the great Mosque at Cordova when I saw for the first time a tartana.

It took possession of me, and in five minutes I had returned the compliment.

It came around the corner with a rush, smothered in a cloud of white dust, in the centre of which I could see the red tassels of the mule and the outstretched arm of the driver seated on the shaft and wielding a whip of convincing length. Then it whirled around before me, backed to the sidewalk, and unloaded half a dozen pairs of black eyes, some mantillas, fans, and red-heeled slippers.

As the fair señoritas were going to mass and I sketching, we separated at once.

A crack of the whip, a plunge from the convinced mule, a dash along a hot, dusty road, bounded by a hedge of prickly pears, and we all stopped at an old Moorish arch, now, as in olden times, one of the city's gates.

I stopped for two reasons. First, because the custom-house officer insisted upon it; and second, because the gate loomed up in such majestic symmetry against the deep blue sky that I determined to paint it at once, and so ordered the driver to unlimber, and prepared for action.

This meant that the mule was unharnessed and tethered in a shady spot, and that I was anchored out by myself in the tartana in the middle of the road, and in the immediate centre of all the traffic of the city's gate.

Any other position, however, would have been useless, for it was the only spot from which I could see through the arch and into the city's streets beyond.

Considering that I and my tartana were public nuisances, the good-nature and forbearance of the populace were remarkable. Every now and then a great string of mules would come to a standstill off my weather bow, the muleteer would slide down from his perch, step forward, peer into my shaded retreat, catch sight of the easel, apologize for disturbing the painter, and then proceed to disentangle his string of quadrupeds as if it was a matter of course and part of his daily routine.

Even the custom-house officers exacting tithes from the hucksters bringing their produce to the city's market, and who at first regarded me with suspicion, became courteous and lent a helping hand in straightening out the continuous procession of donkeys, market carts, wagons, and teams crossing the cool shadow of the arch.

The crowd about my muleless tartana were equally considerate. They stood for hours patient and silent, filled my water-bottle, brought me coffee, and one old Sancho Panza of a farmer even handed me up a great bunch of white grapes. All they wanted in return was a view of the sketch. This I paid, holding it up regularly for their inspection every half hour.

While this busy scene occupied the roadway under the gate, another of quite a different character was taking place in the grated rooms above it.

I had noticed on my arrival a thinly constructed military gentleman all sword and moustache, who watched me from a window, and who seemed to take an especial interest in my movements. I now caught sight of him at an upper window gesticulating wildly and surrounded by a group of other military gentlemen, all apparently absorbed in me, my tartana, and my circle of art students. Then they disappeared, and I gave the incident no further thought.

Half an hour later the vista of the street seen through the gate, and consequently the central point of my sketch, was obstructed by a mass of people crowding about the great swinging doors, and from it marched a file of soldiers under command of an officer who began a series of military movements of great simplicity.

First, they marched up the road and left two men. Then they marched back and left two more. Then they deployed in front and stationed one at each wheel of my tartana, and finally the officer stepped forward, drew his sword, and, looking me searchingly in the face, made this startling announcement:—

"Señor, the general in command has ordered your instant arrest. You will accompany me to the prison."

As soon as I recovered my breath I came down Jacob's ladder and asked politely for an explanation. The only reply was a crisp order closing the files, followed by a forward march which swept me down the dusty road under the gate, through an iron-barred door, up a broad flight of stone steps leading up one side of the gate-way, and into a room on the second floor dimly lighted by small grated windows.

As soon as my eyes, dazzled by the glare of the sunlight, became accustomed to the semi-darkness, I discovered an officer with snow-white hair and moustache, seated at a desk and poring over a mass of papers. He was in full uniform, was half covered with medals, and attended by a secretary.

He arose, perforated me with his eye, listened to the officer's statement, and demanded my age, name, and occupation. To these questions I gave civil answers, which the secretary recorded.

Then he faced me sternly and said, "What are you doing in Cordova?"

"A little of everything, your excellency. I prowl about the streets, lounge in the cafés, go to mass, make love to the señoritas, attend the bull-fight, and" —

"And make drawings?"

"I admit it, your excellency."

"What do you do with these drawings, señor pintor?"

"Sell them, your excellency — when I can."

"You are a Frenchman?"

"No, I am an American."

"Your passport."

"I have none."

That settled it. Seizing a pen, he indorsed a paper handed him by his secretary, passed it to the officer, and said, in a gruff voice, "Conduct this man to the Governor."

More closing in of files, more drawn sword, more forward march, and down the stone stairs we all tramped, out into the glare of the sunlight, through the excited, sympathetic, and curious mob, and then up on the other side of the gate, and up a precisely similar staircase, and into a precisely similar semi-dark room. More desk, more secretary, — two this time, — and more excellency, but here the similarity ends.

At a square table covered with books and papers was seated a young officer, scarcely twenty years of age, also in full uniform, but without the numismatic collection decorating his chest. He was occupied in rolling a cigarette.

The only sign he gave of our presence was a glance at the squad and a slight nod to the officer, who saluted him with marked deference. As for myself, I do not think I came within his range.

The cigarette complete, he struck a light, blew a cloud of smoke from his nostrils, read the much-indorsed paper, reached for a pen, and was about to countersign it when I stepped forward.

"Will your highness inform me why I am under arrest?"

"Certainly; you have been detected in making plans of this prison, which is a military post of Spain. In time of war this is punished with death; in time of peace, by imprisonment."

All this, you know, with as much ease and grace of manner as if he had invited me to luncheon, and was merely giving directions about the temperature of the burgundy!

"But I am not a spy. I am simply an American painter traveling through Spain, sketching as I go, and painting whatever pleases my fancy. Last week it was the awnings over the street of the Sierpes in Seville, yesterday the donkeys dozing in the sun at the gate of the Mosque, and to-day this old Moorish arch, so typical of Spain's great history."

He threw away his cigarette, lost his languid air, took up the paper, re-read it carefully to the end, and said:—

"But you have no passport."

"You are mistaken."

"Produce it."

I ran my hand into my blouse and handed him my pocket sketch-book.

He opened it, stopped at the first page, turned the others slowly, backed unconsciously into his chair, sat down, covered his face with a smile, broke into a laugh, ordered the officer to follow him, and disappeared through a door.

I occupied myself examining the brass numbers on the cartridge-boxes of the squad, and wondering what size handcuffs I wore. Before I had settled it, the officer returned, saluted me, escorted me through the door, leaving the squad behind, and led me into a small room luxuriously furnished. The young Governor came forward and held out his hand.

"Señor, you are free. I have seen your picture. It is admirable. I regret the mistake. The officer will conduct you to your tartana and detail a file of men who will prevent your being disturbed until you finish. Adios."

It was a noble and goodly sight to see that awkward squad mount guard in the dust and heat! It was so frightfully hot out there in the road, and so delightfully cool inside the tartana. It was another exhilarating exhibition to watch the crowd and see them tortured by hopeless curiosity to understand the situation. It was still an additional delightful spectacle to contemplate the driver, who had shrunk into a mere ghost of himself when the arrest was made, and who was now swelling with the importance of the result.

An hour later the sketch was finished, the squad dismissed, the officer, who turned out to be a charming fellow, was seated beside me; the mule, the driver, and the tartana became once more a compact organization, and we rattled back through the blinding dust, and stopped at a café of the officer's choosing.

Over the cognac I mustered up courage to ask him this question: —

"If you will permit me, señor capitan, who is the young Governor?"

"Do you not know?"

I expressed my ignorance.

"The Governor, caballero, is the cousin of the King."

A VERANDA IN THE ALCAZARIA

To really understand and appreciate Spanish life you must live in the streets. Not lounge through them, but sit down somewhere and keep still long enough for the ants to crawl over you, and so contemplate the people at your leisure. If you are a painter you will have every facility given you. The balconies over your head will be full of señoritas fanning lazily and peering at you through the iron gratings; the barber across the way will lay aside his half-moon basin and cross over to your side of the street and chat with you about the bull-fight of yesterday and the fiesta to-morrow, and give you all the scandal of the neighborhood before noon. The sombrerero, whose awnings are hung with great strings of black hats of all shapes and sizes, will leave his shop and watch you by the hour; and the fat, good-natured priest will stand quietly at your elbow and encourage you with such appreciative criticisms as "Muybien." "Bonita, señor." "Bonisima."

If you keep your eyes about you, you will catch Figaro casting furtive glances at a shaded window above you, and later on a scrap of paper will come fluttering down at your feet, which the quick-witted barber covers with his foot, slyly picks up, and afterwards reads and kisses behind the half-closed curtains of his shop. So much of this sort of thing will go on during the day that you wonder what the night may bring forth.

The Alcazaria in Seville, upon the broad flags of which I spent the greater part of three days, is just such a street. It is a narrow, winding, crooked thoroughfare, shaded by great awnings stretched between the overhanging roofs, and filled with balconies holding great tropical plants, strings of black hats, festoons of gay colored stuffs, sly peeping señoritas, fruit sellers, aguadores, donkeys, beggars, and the thousand and one things that make up Spanish life.

Before I finished my picture I had become quite an old settler, and knew what time the doctor came in, and who was sick over the way, and the name of the boy with the crutch, and the picador who lived in the rear and who strutted about on the flagging in his buckskin leggings, padded with steel springs, on the day of the bullfight, and the story about the sad-faced girl in the window over the wine shop, whose lover was in prison.

But of course one cannot know a street at one sitting. The Alcazaria, on the morning of the first day, was to me only a Spanish street; on the morning of the second day I began to realize that it contained a window over my shoulder opening on a small veranda half hidden in flowers and palms; and on the morning of the third day I knew just the hour at which its occupant returned from mass, the shape of her head and mantilla, and could recognize her duenna at sight.

This charming Spanish beauty greatly

interested me. If I accidentally caught her eye through the leaves and flowers, she would drop her lashes so quickly, and with such a half frightened, timid look, that I immediately looked the other way for full five minutes in lieu of an apology; and I must confess that after studying her movements for three days I should as soon have thought of kissing my hand to the Mother Superior of the convent as to this modest little maiden. I must also confess that no other señorita led me to any such conclusion in any of the other balconies about me.

On the afternoon of the third day I began final preparations for my departure, and as everybody wanted to see the picture, it was displayed in the shop of the barber because he had a good light. Then I sent his small boy for my big umbrella and for a large, unused canvas which I had stored in the wine shop at the corner, and which, with my smaller traps, he agreed to take to my lodgings; and then there was a general hand-shaking and some slight waving of white hands and handkerchiefs from the balconies over the way, in which my timid señorita did not join; and so, lighting my cigarette, I made my adios and strolled down the street to the church.

It was the hour for vespers, and the streets were filling rapidly with penitents on their way to prayers. With no definite object in view except to see the people and watch their movements, and with that sense of relief which comes over one after his day's work is done, I mingled in the throng and passed between the great swinging doors and into the wide incense-laden interior, and sat down near the door to watch the service. The dim light sifted in through the stained-glass windows and rested on the clouds of incense swung from the censers. Every now and then I heard the tinkling of the altar-bell, and the deep tones of the organ. Around me were the bowed heads of the penitents, silently telling their beads, and next me the upturned face and streaming eyes of a grief-stricken woman, whispering her sorrow to the Virgin. To the left of where I kneeled was a small chapel, and, dividing me from this, an iron grating of delicate workmanship, behind which were grouped a number of people praying before a picture of the Christ. Suddenly another figure came in, kneeled, and prayed silently. It was my timid señorita, and before I was through wondering how she could come so quickly, a young priest entered and knelt immediately behind her. He was the same I had seen in the Alcazaria glancing at her window as he passed.

Fearing that I should frighten her, as I had often done before, I moved a few steps away; but she was so lovely and Madonna-like with her mantilla shading her eyes and her fan fluttering slowly like a butterfly, — now poising, now balancing, then waving and settling, — that I instinctively sought for my sketch-book to catch an outline of her pose, feeling assured that I should not be discovered. Before I had half finished she arose, slowly passed the priest, half covered him with her mantilla, and quick as thought slipped a white envelope under his prayer-book!

It was done so neatly and quickly and with such self-possession that it was some time before I recovered my equilibrium. Had I made any mistake? Could it possibly be the same demure, modest, shy señorita of the veranda, or was it not some one resembling her? All these Spanish beauties have black eyes, I thought, carry the colors of their favorite matador on their fans, and look alike. Perhaps, after all, I was mistaken.

I determined to find out.

Before she had reached the outer step of the church I had overtaken her, but her mantilla was too closely drawn for me to see her face. The duenna, however, was unmistakable, for she wore great silver hoops in her ears and an enormously high comb, and once seen was not easily forgotten; but to be quite sure, I followed along until she entered the Alcazaria, and so on to the step of her house. If she touched the old Moorish knocker and rapped, it would end it.

She lingered for a few minutes at the iron gate, chatted with her duenna, watched me cross the street, kept her eyes upon me with her old saintly look, patted her attendant on the back, gently closed the gate upon the good woman, leaving her on the inside, then bent her own pretty head, pushed back her mantilla, showing her white throat, and flashing upon me from the corner of her eye the most coquettish, daring, and mischievous of glances, touched her finger-tips to her lips, and vanished!

I had made no mistake except in human nature. Surely Murillo must have gone to Italy for his Madonnas. They were not in Seville, if the times have not changed.

I crossed over and had a parting chat with the barber. What about the señorita opposite who had just entered her gate? "Ah, señor! She is most lovely. She is called The Pious; but you need not look that way. She is the betrothed of the olive merchant who lives at San Juan, and who visits her every Sunday. The wedding takes place next month."

Figaro believed it. I could see it in his face. So, perhaps, did the olive merchant.

I did not.

IN AND OUT OF A CAB IN AMSTERDAM

It is raining this morning in Amsterdam. It is a way it has in Holland. The old settlers do not seem to mind it, but I am only a few days from the land of the orange and the olive, and, although these wet, silvery grays and fresh greens are full of "quality," I long for the deep blue skies and clear-cut shadows of sunny Spain. On this particular morning I am in a cab and in search of a certain fish-market, and cabby is following the directions given him by a very round porter with a very flat cap and a deep bass voice.

There is nothing so comfortable as a cab to paint in if you only know how to utilize its resources. For me, long practice has brought it to a fine art. First, I have cabby take out the horse. This prevents his shaking me when he changes his tired leg. He is generally a spiral-spring-fed beast, and enjoys the relief. Then I take out the cushions. This keeps them dry. Then I close the back and off-side curtains, so as to concentrate the light, prop my easel up against the front seat, spread my palette and brushes on the bare wooden one, hang my rubber water-bottle up to the arm rest, and begin work. (I have even discovered in the bottom of certain cabs such luxuries as knot or auger holes through which to pour my waste water.) I then pass the umbrella-staff to cabby, calling particular attention to the iron spike, and explain how useful it may become in removing the inquisitive small boy from the hind wheel. One lesson and two boys makes a cabby an expert. This is why I am in a cab and am driving down the Keizersgraacht on this very wet morning in Amsterdam.

Before the fat porter's directions could be fully carried out, however, I caught sight of an old bridge spanning a canal which pleased me greatly, and before my friend on the box could realize the consequences I had his horse out and tied to a wharf post, and the interior of his cab transformed into a studio.

In five minutes I discovered that a cabless horse and a horseless cab presided over by a cabby armed with an umbrella-staff was not an every-day sight in Amsterdam. I had camped on the stone quay some distance from the street and out of everybody's way. I congratulated myself on my location, and felt sure I would not be disturbed. On my left was the canal crowded with market-boats laden with garden-truck; on my right, the narrow street choked with the traffic of the city.

Suddenly the business of Amsterdam ceased. Everybody on the large boats scrambled into smaller ones and sculled for shore. Everybody in the street simultaneously jumped from cart, wagon, and doorstep, and in twenty seconds I was overwhelmed by a surging throng, who swarmed about my four-wheeler and blocked up my only window with anxious, inquiring faces.

I had been in a crowd like this before, and knew exactly what to do. Sphynx-like silence and immobility of face are imperative. If you neither speak nor smile, the mob imbibes a kind of respect for you amounting almost to awe. Those nearest you, who can see a little and want to see more, unconsciously become your champions, and expostulate with those who cannot see anything, cautioning them against shaking the painter and obstructing his view.

This crowd was no exception to the general rule. I noticed, however, one peculiarity. As each Amsterdammer reached my window he would gaze silently at my canvas and then say, "Ah, teekenmeester." Soon the word went around and reached the belated citizens rushing up, who stopped and appeared satisfied, as they all exclaimed, "Ah, teekenmeester."

At last commerce resumed her sway. The street disentangled itself. The market in cabbages again became active, and I was left comparatively alone, always excepting the small boy. The variety here was singularly irritating. They mounted the roof, blocked up the windows, clambered up on the front seat, until cabby became sufficiently conversant with the use of the business end of my umbrella-staff, after which they kept themselves at a respectful distance.

Finally a calm settled down over everything. The rain fell gently and continuously. The spiral-spring beast rested himself on alternate legs, and the boys contemplated me from a distance. Cabby leaned in the off window and became useful as a cup holder, and I was rapidly finishing my first sketch in Holland when the light was shut out, and looking up I saw the head of an officer of police. He surveyed me keenly, — my sketch and my interior arrangements, — and then in a gruff voice gave me an order in low Dutch. I pointed to my staff holder, and continued painting. In a moment the officer thrust his head through the off window and repeated his order in high Dutch. I waved him away firmly, and again referred him to cabby.

Then a war began on the outside in which everybody took a hand, and in half a minute more the population of Amsterdam had blocked up the wharf. I preserved my Egyptian exterior, and proceeded unconcernedly to lay a fresh wash over my sky. While thus occupied, I became conscious that the spiral-spring was being united once more to the cab. This fact became positive when cabby delivered up the umbrella-staff and opened the door.

I got out.

The gentleman in gilt buttons was at a white heat. The mass-meeting were indulging in a running fire of criticism, punctuated by loose cabbage leaves and rejected vegetables, which sailed, bomb-like, through the air, and the upshot of the whole matter was that the officer ordered me away from the quay and into a side street.

But why? The streets of Amsterdam were free. I was out of everybody's way, was breaking no law, and creating no disturbance.

At this instant half of a yesterday's cabbage came sailing through the atmosphere from a spot in the direction of a group of wharf-rats, struck the officer's helmet, and rolled it into the canal. A yell went up from the crowd, cabby went down to the water for the headgear, and the owner drew his short sword and charged on the wharf-rats, who suddenly disappeared.

I reëntered my studio, shut the door, and continued work. I concluded that it was not my funeral.

I remember distinctly the situation at this moment. I had my water-bottle in my hand re-filling the cups, mouth full of brushes, palette on my lap, and easel steadied by one foot. Suddenly a face surmounted by a wet helmet, and livid with rage, was thrust into mine, and a three-cornered variety of dialect that would produce a sore throat in any one except a Dutchman was hurled at me, accompanied by the usual well-known "move on" gesture.

Remembering the soothing influence exerted on the former mob, I touched my hat to his excellency, and said, "Teekenmeester." The head disappeared like a shot, and in an instant I was flat on my back in the bottom of the cab, bespattered with water, smeared with paint, and half smothered under a débris of cushions, water-cups, wet-paper, and loose sketches, and in that position was unceremoniously jolted over the stones.

The majesty of the law had asserted itself! I was backed up in a side street!

I broke open the door and crawled out in the rain. His excellency was standing at the head of the spiral-spring, with a sardonic grin on his countenance.

The mob greeted my appearance with a shout of derision. I mounted the driver's seat and harangued them. I asked, in a voice which might have been heard in Rotterdam, if anybody about me understood English. A shabbily-dressed, threadbare young fellow elbowed his way towards me and said he did. I helped him up beside me on the box and addressed the multitude, my seedy friend interpreting. I reviewed the history of old Amsterdam and its traditions; its reputation for hospitality; its powerful colonies scattered over the world; its love for art and artists. Then I passed to the greatest of all its possessions, — the New Amsterdam of the New World, my own city, — and asked them as Amsterdammers, or the reverse, whether they considered I had been fairly treated in the city of my great-grandfathers —I, a painter and a New Yorker!

I had come three thousand miles to carry home to their children in the New World some sketches of the grand old city they loved so well, and in return I had been insulted, abused, bumped over the stones, and made a laughing stock.

I would appeal to them as brothers to decide whether these streets of Amsterdam were not always open to her descendants, and whether I was not entitled to use them at all times by virtue of my very birthright. (Another shout went up, but this time a friendly one.) This being the case, I proposed to reoccupy my position and finish my sketch. If I had violated any law it was the duty of the officer to put me under arrest. If not, then I was free to do as I pleased; and if the highly honorable group of influential citizens about me would open their ranks, I would drive the cab back myself to the spot from which I had been so cruelly torn.

Another prolonged shout followed the interpretation, an opening was quickly made, and I had begun to chafe the spiral-spring with my shabby friend's umbrella, when cabby rushed forward, pale and trembling, seized the bridle, and begged me piteously to desist. My friend then explained that cabby would probably lose his license if I persisted, although I might carry my point and his cab back to the quay.

This argument being unanswerable, a a council of war was held, to which a number of citizens who were leaning over the front wheels were invited, and it was decided to drive at once to the nearest police station and submit the whole outrage to the chief.

In two minutes we halted under the traditional green glass lamp so familiar to all frequenters of such places. We saluted the sergeant, and were shown up a winding iron staircase into a small room and up to a long green table, behind which sat a baldheaded old fellow in undress uniform, smoking a short pipe.

My threadbare friend explained the cause of our visit. The old fellow looked surprised, and touched a bell which brought in another smoker in full dress, whose right ear served as a rack for a quill pen, and who used it (the pen not the ear) to take down our statement. Then the chief turned to me and asked my name. I gave it. This he repeated to the secretary. Occupation? Painter. "Teekenmeester," said he to the secretary.

Magic word! I have you at last. Teekenmeester is Dutch for painter.

The chief read the secretary's notes, signed them, and said I should call again in ten days, and he would submit a report.

"Report! What do I want with a report, your imperial highness? It is now four o'clock, and I have but two hours of daylight to finish this sketch. I don't want a report. I want an order compelling the pirate who presides over the cabbage market district to respect the rights of a descendant of Amsterdam who is peacefully pursuing his avocation." Certainly, he so intended. I was at liberty to replace my cab and finish my sketch. The officer exceeded his instructions.

But how? I did not want either to provoke a riot or get my cabby into trouble. Ah, he understood. Another bell brought an orderly, who conducted us down-stairs, opened a side door, called two officers, placed one outside with cabby and the other inside with me and Threadbare, and we drove straight back to the quay and were welcomed by a shout from my constituents compared to which all former cheering was a dead silence. I looked around for his excellency, but he was nowhere to be seen.

Verily, the majesty of the law had asserted itself!

I do not think I made much of an impression as a painter in Amsterdam, but I have always had an idea that I could be elected alderman in the cabbage market district.

A WATER-LOGGED TOWN IN HOLLAND

HAVING shaken the water of Amsterdam from off my feet, dust being out of the question in this moist climate, I have settled myself for a month in this sleepy old town of Dordrecht on the Maas.

It is a fair sample of all Holland, — flat, wet, and quaint; full of canals, market boats, red-tiled roofs, rosy-cheeked girls, brass milk cans, wooden shoes, and fish. Every inch of it is as clean as bare arms, scrubbing brushes, and plenty of water can make it. The town possesses an old gate built in fifteen hundred and something, a Groote Kerk built before America was discovered, and several old houses constructed immediately thereafter, together with the usual assortment of bridges, dikes, market-places, and windmills.

I lodge in two rooms at the top of a crooked staircase, and as three sides of my apartments overlook the Maas I see a constant procession of Dutch luggers, Rhine steamers, and fishing smacks. When it rains I paint from one of my windows. When it shines I am along the canals or drifting over to Papendrecht, or at work under the trees which fringe every street.

My fellow lodgers afford me infinite enjoyment. There is a doctor who does not practice, a merchant who does no business, and mine host who is everybody's friend, and who attends to everything in his own section of the town, including his inn.

Then there is Johan. He is porter, interpreter, guide, boots, railway agent, postal official, head waiter, and cook. He assumes and sustains all these various personages simply by the changes possible with a white apron, a railway badge, and two kinds of caps, — one flat and the other round-topped.

For instance, when you arrive at the

brisk little station of Dort, kept permanently awake by the noise of constantly passing trains, Johan is waiting for you, wearing his flat-topped cap and porter's badge, and has your luggage on his handcart before you know it.

Or perhaps at dinner you ask the demure old butler for more boiled fish, and on looking closely and trying to recall his face, you are startled to recognize your friend at the station who handled your trunk. Johan enjoys your puzzled look. He knows it is simply a question of a slightly bald head and white apron in exchange for a flat cap and a badge.

Later on you ask for a guide who speaks your own language, whatever that may be. A jaunty fellow presents himself holding his round-topped cap in his hand, and is prepared to show you the universe. It is Johan.

Besides this, he speaks the fag ends of six languages, all with a strong Dutch accent. He says to me, " It will some rain more as yesterday,—don't it?" This is why I know he is a linguist.

Last of all there is Sophy, who is maid of all work. She it is who cares for my

A Water-Logged Town in Holland

rooms, sews on my buttons, wakes me in the morning, and washes my brushes. She is a rosy-cheeked girl of twenty, wears a snow white cap (screwed to her head with two gold spirals), short skirts, blue yarn stockings, and white wooden shoes; and is never still one minute that she is awake.

Moreover, she has a pair of arms as red as apples and about the size of a blacksmith's, which she uses with a flail-like movement that makes her dangerous. Every paving-stone, door-step, window-sill, and pane of glass within the possession of mine host knows all about this pair of arms, for Sophy first souses them with great pails of water, which she herself dips from the canal, and then polishes them with a coarse towel until they shine all over. She has a mortal antipathy to dirt and a high regard for Johan, whom she looks upon as a superior being.

These are my simple surroundings in this water-logged town. I have only one drawback. I do not speak its liquid dialect.

UNDER A BALCONY.

Behind the Groote Kerk is a moss-grown landing-place, shaded by a row of trees, the trunks of which serve as moorings for some broad Dutch luggers floating idly in the sluggish canal. Away up among the branches are their topmasts half hidden amidst the leaves. Across this narrow strip of water is thrown a slender foot bridge to a row of reddish brown houses running Venetian-like sheer into the canal, with their overhanging balconies and windows filled with gay flowers in bright China pots.

I have already become quite intimate with the domestic affairs of some of the inmates of these houses.

One three-windowed balcony especially interests me. I have never seen flowers require so much water. Every time I look up from my easel she drops her eyes and pours on another pitcher. And then the pruning and trimming is something marvelous! She is a bright little body with big blue eyes, and the tangled vines and flowers climbing over the quaint wooden window make a charming frame for her pretty face.

It is difficult to paint under such circumstances, and if I over-elaborated the details of this balcony in my sketch, I frankly say I could not help it.

Suddenly she disappears, and in her place stands a pleasant-faced young Hollander, having the air of a student, who makes me a slight bow which I gladly return, for I am anxious to prove to him how honorable have been my intentions.

In a few moments my fair window-gardener comes tripping over the bridge bearing a small tray, which, to my great astonishment, she lays at my feet on the clean flagging.

She makes no reply to my thanks except with her eyes, and, before I am half through with my little speech, is over the bridge and out of sight.

The tray contains some thin slices of cheese, a few biscuits, and a pot of milk. This is almost immediately followed by the student himself, who holds out his hand heartily, which I grasp, and who addresses me in Dutch, accompanied by those peculiar nods and frowns common to all of us when we are sure we are not understood. I sadly shake my head.

Then he tries Italian. I shrug my shoulders in a hopeless way.

"Perhaps, sir, then, it may be that you speak some English?" I wanted to fall upon his neck.

"Speak English, my dear sir? It is my favorite language. Let us converse in English, by all means. But where did you learn it?"

"Here in Dordrecht. Where did you?"

"I? Oh, in America. My mother spoke it perfectly."

"How interesting! I was not aware you Spaniards spoke it with so little accent. I do not speak Spanish myself, for which I am truly sorry. It is so musical."

Now that was very kind of him. I knew that I had absorbed during my two months' residence in Spain something of the air of an Hidalgo, but I was not prepared for this!

He was glad to make the acquaintance of a Spanish painter. He so much admired our school. He had been in his study and had watched me all the morning, and finding me still at work at lunch hour had taken the liberty of sending his sister

A Water-Logged Town in Holland   65

with the tray. It was a leisure month with him, the college being closed. He would like to watch me paint, especially now that he knew his own windows formed part of the picture.

An hour later the pretty sister is filling his pipe and my empty cup in a cosy little room with windows filled with flowers, through which I can see my sketching ground of the morning.

She has donned another cap more bewitching than the first and is busying herself about the room. It is a cosy little den, and rests you to sit in it. The walls are lined with shelves, laden with books. The tables are covered with French, English, and German magazines, pamphlets, and papers. A student's lamp, a few rare etchings, some choice bits of porcelain, and three or four easy chairs complete the interior.

While we smoke my host begs me tell him something of Spain and my people, and when I undeceive him as to my nationality he laughs heartily, and is doubly glad to make the discovery, for now that he knows I hail from one of the colonies I am of course a kinsman of his. He explains that he had mistaken me for a Spaniard because as he watched me from his study window he noticed that I smoked cigarettes and twisted my moustache!

Late in the afternoon when I knock the ashes from my third pipe he insists on accompanying me to my boat, and before we part we exchange cards and arrange for a little dinner at my rooms the next day *for three.*

Verily a white umbrella is better than a Letter of Credit!

As soon as I reached my lodgings I sent for Johan and handed him my host's card. "Who is that gentleman?" His eyes opened very wide. "Dot yentleman? Dot yentleman, Mynheer, is the professor of English at the university."

A DAY WITH THE PROFESSOR.

I tell the professor he is a godsend to me, for while I am all ears and eyes and have something of a nose for poking into odd places, he supplies me with a tongue, which completes my equipment. He returns the compliment by saying I am the only gentleman speaking English he has ever met, and that his pronunciation is improving daily. I remark to him that either Englishmen or politeness have been very scarce in Dordrecht heretofore, at which he laughs and says he shall never overcome all the peculiarities of my language.

Under his guidance I have ransacked every crook, cranny, and sluiceway in this curious old town. This morning being Friday, we go to the market. It is a small open square on one side of the Voorstraat. It is really the floor of a great stone bridge, for the canal runs beneath it.

In every town in Holland on market day you will find two stalls which may interest you, — one is the junkman's, who sells old iron, hinges, locks, and broken kitchen ware, and sometimes rusty swords, fragments of armor, and rare old brass and copper utensils, battered and bruised. The other contains old books, engravings, and prints.

Successive Friday mornings have added to my own stock of bric-a-brac, but this morning it is the professor who hugs all the way back to my improvised studio three great Dutch books for which he says he has looked for months.

He wondered yesterday why I stopped the milkmaid on the street and bought her heirloom of a milk-can covered with scars and patches and shining like gold, but to-day he is even more astonished at the miscellaneous assortment of rusty iron hinges, locks, and handles I have picked out, and which with the assistance of an aged locksmith and his wife will soon be restored to their pristine polish.

But I have an old Dutch cabinet at home which has waited for these irons for years, and the milk-can exactly fits the shelf on the top.

He raves, however, about these old books; tells me that Mynheer somebody or other, whose name is full of *o*'s and *j*'s, wrote this treatise in the last century, and that there has been a great dispute about it; that a spurious edition was published which at one time was accepted; that he had looked for the original for many months. Then he removes his pipe, blows the blue smoke out of my window, and fondly pats the cover.

I think to myself as I look at him with his high forehead, deep, keen eyes, and thoughtful look, what a thorough Bohemian he would have made if he had only taken to paint and bric-a-brac instead of languages and literature.

The clack of Sophy's wooden shoes hurrying up-stairs announces breakfast, which Johan serves with more than usual solemnity owing to the professor's presence, and also to the fact that for three days no one has arrived at our inn, and consequently his attention has not been diverted from his table to the duties of either porter, railway official, or guide.

This over, Sophy clatters across the clean cobbles to the stone quay, and bales the rain of last night from my boat, and the professor and I drift down the Wagensluis to where some overhanging balconies shelter from the sun and rain an old barge, the bow of which serves as a foreground for a sketch I am finishing of the canal with the Groote Kerk in the distance. While I paint he smokes and reads, and nods to the passing boats, and tells me stories of the people about us and the current gossip of the town, and so the hours slip by.

Then, as the shadows lengthen and my work is over, we row back and out on the broad Maas, and watch the sun set behind the big windmill at Papendrecht, and the Dutch luggers anchored in pairs in midstream waiting for a change in the tide to float them to Rotterdam and a market.

When the sun goes down and it becomes quite dark we drift back, picking our way among the market boats moored for the night along the quays, and up to a flight of wooden steps slippery with ooze and slime and well known to both of us. It is the nearest landing to a small beer house which we frequent.

The landlord greets us heartily, and takes down two pewter-topped mugs from a row against the wall, and spreads a clean cloth over one of the tables overlooking the dark canal with its flickering mast-head lights and deep shadows.

Before we can blow the froth from our mugs the landlord returns with a dish of cold boiled potatoes, some leaves of lettuce, and the castors, and the professor proceeds with great gravity to peel and slice, pour on the oil and vinegar, adding a pinch of salt, and finishing the whole with crisp sprigs of lettuce, which he plants here and there on the top.

A cup of coffee, cigarettes, and pipes, a few strokes of the oars, and I bid the professor good-night at the landing nearest his house, and so on to mine.

Johan thrusts his head from the side window at my third ring, unlocks the door, and lights for me a slender candle. As I climb the crooked staircase, I overhear him yawning and muttering to himself, "Dot veller von America shleep notting."

A VISIT FROM THE DOCTOR.

From the windows of my rooms I can see the only busy spot in all Dordrecht. It is the wharf immediately beneath me, where all the Rhine steamers land, and which is crowded all day long with groups of people either going to or coming from the different small towns and villages up and down this outlet to the sea.

On rainy days I draw the curtains wide apart, fasten back the shutters, set up my easel, and pick out a subject from the moving panorama below. The wharf is piled high with garden truck in huge wicker baskets, boxes of fish, rows of brass milk cans reflecting their polished sides in the wet pavements, furniture, crates of crockery, and the usual assortment of small merchandise. On its wet planks the leave-takings and welcomings occur every half hour; that is, upon the arrival and departure of each boat, and during the whole day it seems as if all the vitality and energy of Dordrecht had concentrated itself under my window. Elsewhere the town is fast asleep.

Out on the Maas the lazy luggers with their red and white sails float by, the skipper's wife usually holding the tiller. Across the marshes the sails of the windmills turn lazily as if it were an exertion for them to move, and over all falls the gentle rain.

On these days I have many knocks at my door announcing various visitors. The doctor generally drops in early. He is a cheery old soul, and although he speaks very little English, I have picked up enough broken Dutch to piece out with, and so we get on very well. His picturesque faded green coat, yellow nankeen waistcoat, and red necktie make him very valuable around a studio.

Then he is never in the way. He raps,

opens the door, sees me, shuts it, raps again gently, and then comes in with an air of surprise mingled with genuine delight at finding me, fills his pipe from my tobacco-box, spreads himself on my lounge, and smokes away quietly.

I would love him for this quality alone, even if he had no other, — for it is a rare kind of man who can come noiselessly into your studio when you are at work, dispense with more than a nod of greeting, slide into a seat, help himself to a pipe, and so unconsciously become one of your surroundings.

Besides, the doctor is especially interested in the small collection of old brass, hammered iron, and bric-a-brac I have made since my sojourn with them all at the inn, and which is scattered about my room, and he takes the greatest delight in examining each new addition that I make.

To-day he is brimful. He has heard of a man who lives on the quay near the potato market, just returned from Friesland, who has enough old Dutch leather to cover the walls of my two rooms, and all perfect and of one pattern, and very cheap!

I look incredulous, and hint that so

much leather of one pattern did not exist in all Holland outside of a museum, and perhaps not in one. But he will not listen. He insists that the man bought the whole house, and then pulled it to pieces for the leather which lined the walls of one room. The potato market was close by, the rain was nearly over, and I must go with him at once. I knew the potato market and the quay, for I had painted them the week before with a pretty milk girl carrying her cans across the foreground of my picture. So to oblige him I take down my storm coat from its peg, and we tramp through the wet streets to the market and up to a small house, the front of which is built on an angle, so that the third story windows lean over the sidewalk. This enables the occupants to see who comes in the front door without going down-stairs,— not an unusual style of house, by the way, in Holland.

"Would Mynheer show the painter from America the leather he had in the garret?"

Mynheer at first did not have any leather at all in the garret; then he had only a few pieces, but they were not there; then he could get some more if we would call the next day.

But this did not suit the doctor. He knew all about it. He had a friend who had *seen* it. Mynheer need not expect to keep the leather for the rich Englishman. The American painter would pay more.

At this the old Shylock led the way up an almost perpendicular staircase. The doctor was right. There lay the leather in flat sheets and of a quality and quantity that proved the truth of the whole story, but the price demanded would have ruined the American painter.

On the way home the old fellow built up and destroyed a dozen schemes by which I was to get the leather at half its value or my own price, none of which would have been possible without the permission of the police.

The next morning a much softer knock than usual announces the good doctor, wearing so sad a face that I fear some calamity has overtaken him. He only shakes his head and puffs away. Then it leaks out that on his way to the post he had seen Shylock packing on the sidewalk a long, wide, flat box, marked London. The Englishman had bought the leather.

Since then the doctor often starts up from my lounge after a long reverie, knocks the ashes from his pipe, lays his hand upon my shoulder, looks at me sadly, and says, "Dot Englishman!" And then goes out shaking his head ominously. Incidents like these in my quiet life at this charming old inn make even rainy days pleasant in Dordrecht.

ON THE RIVA, VENICE

My gondolier, Ingenio, is a wrinkled old sea-dog, with gray hair and stooping shoulders, who has the air of a retired buccaneer and the voice of a girl. His gondola has been my home for a month past, and he has been my constant companion. As he speaks nothing but Italian and I nothing resembling it, we have adopted a sign language which answers perfectly. This morning he comes through the garden where I am taking my coffee, points to his gondola floating at the foot of the marble steps leading to the Grand Canal, touches his forehead, then his pocket, holds up two fingers and motions as if to sit down. I understand at once that he has thought of a new shop where for a few francs we can buy two antique chairs, of a pattern especially desired by me.

These chairs have greatly bothered Ingenio. Under the plea of searching for them, I have ransacked half the old palaces in Venice, and have discovered most marvelous rooms, with ceilings of carved beams edged with gilt, with faded frescoes, exquisite marble staircases leading thereto, and often quaint and picturesque interiors inhabited by the present generation.

I have, of course, found every variety of chair, old and new, but the search has been so delightful, and the discoveries have partaken so much of the unexpected, that I refuse to be satisfied with any of them, and so continue my explorations; Ingenio poking the nose of his gondola into every crooked canal in Venice, and I my own up one half of her equally crooked staircases and across many an old courtyard and damp, mould-covered garden.

But this morning I shook my head, which was full of another and a more brilliant idea, — an idea which I conveyed to Ingenio by pointing down the canal with my umbrella staff, putting up my hands like a little praying Samuel, and sketching an imaginary bridge on the tablecloth with my coffee spoon.

Ingenio understood at once. He knew

that I wanted to paint the bridge near the old church on the Riva degli Schiavoni.

In five minutes we were floating past the Piazza and San Marco, and in as many more had reached the quay near the Church of the Santa Maria della Pieta.

I had seen a group of fishing boats moored here as I drifted past the afternoon before, and I reasoned that, as the tide did not change until noon, there was, perhaps, time to catch them before they spread their gorgeous wings of red and gold and flew away to their homes in Chioggia.

We landed at the small piazza which formed the quay, at the end of which ran a flight of marble steps up and over the bridge. To the left of this were moored the boats with all sails set, hanging listless in the still air. In front was the white marble pavement baking in the sun.

I soon found the open door of the Santa Maria was my only shelter from the blinding heat. By hugging one side of the porch, and resting one leg of my easel against the lower hinge, I was sheltered in the shadow, and could still see the subject of my picture entire. So without more ado, I opened my folding seat and unlimbered my trap, while Ingenio filled the water bottles.

There are so many white umbrellas and floating studios in Venice that an artist at work excites very little curiosity. Occasionally the novelty of my position would tempt some penitent to glance over my shoulder, as she entered the church, making room lest she disturb me, but with this exception I worked on without interruption.

As the heat increased, the worshipers grew less numerous and the quay became nearly deserted. Ingenio, who had gone to sleep in the shadow, was now broiling in the sun, and my left or palette hand felt scorching hot.

But these are trifles when you have two fishing boats half finished, the tide to turn in two hours, and you begin to note the crew already moving about and restlessly handling the ropes. You grow nervous every time a man goes ashore, lest he shall cast off the moorings, and so wreck your morning's work.

Suddenly a sunbeam shot across the upper corner of my canvas. I looked around and up. The sun was slanting over and down the cornice of the church, and with such intensity that I felt an immediate change of base imperative. You cannot see color by the side of a sunbeam.

In Venice, when your best friends fail and life begins to be a burden, you have one resource, — you call for your gondolier. So I awoke Ingenio. He appreciated the situation at once. He ran to the gondola, brought back my large umbrella, and wasted ten minutes of my precious time in attempting to drive its spiked staff into a flight of polished marble steps. The only result was the loss of the spike and the little that remained of my good temper.

After this failure I decided that heroic treatment was all that was left. I first pointed to my half-finished sails, seized the ropes in an imaginary sort of way as if lowering them, and then lifted my hands in despair. Then I gave him two francs, and followed him with my eyes as he disappeared over the bridge and reappeared on the deck of one of the boats.

A row of grinning faces all looked my way, and in a moment more Ingenio returned without the money and with one of the fishermen. The latter gazed silently at my sketch and said, "Buono." I was reassured. The sails were safe, at all events. But the heat continued to be frightful.

Another pantomime then followed with Ingenio, to which the fisherman lent a helping hand. I unfolded my plan slowly and with some misgivings. Ingenio turned a trifle pale and the fisherman looked somewhat alarmed. Five francs more, and a pleasanter expression asserted itself in the latter's face. Then they both measured the distance between the two doors, found an iron hook high up on the mouldings over the arch, returned to the boats, and in five minutes I had rigged an orange-colored jib sail across the entrance of the church, and had crawled in underneath, out of the sun, into its grateful shadow!

I do not offer any apology for this. I distinctly vow that I intended no disrespect to the most holy Maria della Pieta. I was simply backed up into a church door on the sunny side of a quay, with the thermometer in the nineties, an unfinished sketch before me, a marble wall behind me, and but two hours of tide remaining. The effect of a jib sail on Venetian church architecture was not under consideration by me. The possible loss of one in my picture was at the moment of greater importance.

At that instant the horror-stricken and very oily face of a well-fed priest peered into my improvised tent, and from it followed a torrent of Italian. I raised my hat meekly, bowed reverently, and pointed to Ingenio. While the discussion lasted, I managed to finish the rigging, the awning on deck, and the gondola alongside, but the crisis had arrived. I must either take in the jib or go with the priest. This sentiment seemed also to be shared by the crowd. I preferred the latter, and detailing the fisherman to stand by and "repel boarders," I called Ingenio, and followed his oiliness through the cool church, down a long passage, and up to a dark green door heavily hinged and locked.

The priest touched a bell, footsteps were heard, and a sliding panel revealed the sad face of a nun. A word of explanation followed, the bolts were shot back, and I found myself in a small vestibule leading into a low room, white, bare, and scrupulously clean. In a moment more the nun returned, bringing the Mother Superior. I saluted her as if she had been the Queen of Sheba. She listened incredulously to the voluble priest as he elaborated the outrage, and then indignantly turned to Ingenio, who hung his head and chewed the rim of his hat. Then she raised both hands as if in amazement, looked me straight in the face, and slowly shook her head. The sad-faced nun waited, and heard me expostulate in my choicest English that I had the greatest reverence for every church in Italy and for every Lady Superior. I only objected to the climate, and to the fact that this particular church was not on the shady side of the quay.

Then the nun slipped away, and presently returned with a sister in gray, who had the face of a Madonna and the voice of an angel, and an English angel at that. She questioned the priest, then Ingenio, then the sad-faced nun, and then turned to me.

Did the painter speak Italian? Not a word. Furthermore, he was a stranger in a foreign land, away from the home of his childhood, without friends except this poor gondolier, his only possession being a half-finished sketch and a jib sail, for both of which he pleaded.

She listened, half smiling, and said the priest need not remain, and perhaps the gondolier had best return and watch my easel; the good mother need not be alarmed. There was some mistake. She would return to the church with the painter and verify the good priest's story.

I stopped for a moment as she made her devotions at the altar. As we reached the outer door she caught sight of the jib, and stood still as if shocked. My yellow rag was waving in the sunlight as defiant as a matador's cloak!

Stooping under the improvised awning, she closely examined the sketch. How long would it take to finish it? Half an hour. Be quick about it, then. If I did not mind, she would watch me paint. She stood for a long time without speaking, and then said, "Would not a touch of rose madder help that shadow?" "You paint, then?" I asked, following her suggestion. "I did once," she replied, and turned her head sadly and looked out over the blue lagoon towards San Giorgio.

An hour later she watched Ingenio and

the fisherman take down the jib and return it to the boats. But she would not receive my thanks. All artists were her friends. The sail made no difference, the sun was too hot to work without it, and she understood it all when she saw the sketch. She would close the church door. I need not wait. I drifted slowly out into the lagoon and looked back. She was still standing in the archway, shading her eyes with her hand, and watching us.

Then the fishing boats spread their sails, drifted past, and shut her from my sight. Ingenio's cry of warning as he rounded a turn in the canal awoke me from my reverie. I picked up my sketch and stepped ashore. I will give it to any one who will tell me the history of that good gray nun.

A SUMMER'S DAY IN VENICE

Below the Piazza and quite near the Public Garden there is a small wine shop, the open door of which is covered by a striped awning of red and orange. Underneath this at all times of the day and most of the night are collected a group of Italians, who have one object in life which they never lose sight of, — never to do to-day what they can possibly do to-morrow or the next week. If time is money, the average Venetian is a millionaire. He has stored up for present and future use such a vast amount of leisure that it makes a busy man envious to contemplate him.

If you leave your gondola and cross the sun-baked quay to this shelter, these aristocrats will make room for you at their table and hand you a flagon of tepid water and a saucer containing two lumps of sugar; or perhaps the landlord will bring you a bottle of Cerise (cherry juice) and a thin cigar about the size and length of a shoestring. The cigar has a movable backbone of a single broom straw.

Inside of this retreat are small tables, around which are seated other nabobs drinking coffee and playing dominoes. Occasionally one will rise from his seat, approach a high table at one end of the room, select a small bit of dried fish from a pewter platter, and gravely resume his chair with the air of a man who really owned the whole fish, but allowed the landlord to keep it on his sideboard merely as a mark of the high esteem in which he held him.

Should you land immediately opposite the awning and the open door, so as to be quite within sight from the inside, one of these princes will slide from his seat very much as a turtle does from his log and hold your boat steady with his staff until you step ashore. For this service you give him one penny, and quite a small penny at that.

A turn of Ingenio's wrist whirled the sharp blade of my gondola close to this quay one lovely morning in August with results to me exactly similar to what I have described, and in a moment more I was dropping my second lump into the clumsy little cup which the landlord filled from the common pot.

What to paint to-day was the question that bothered me. Should I go back to the Rialto and try the flight of steps up from the canal with the gondolas and boats in the foreground, or the view from the Piazzetta across the small fruit-market with the Great Bridge in the distance, or should I keep on to the Public Gardens and catch the fishing boats as they came across from the Lido?

Ingenio stood by, hat in hand, trying to read my thoughts. It is delightful to watch him. He starts off with a great show of enthusiasm, points up the canal, seizes a cup, turns it upside down, plants a fork beside it, and by this pantomime seeks to recall to me a spot in yesterday's excursion where I halted long enough to make some memoranda of a cluster of mooring piles with the round dome of the Salute in the distance.

"No? Bah! Certainly not; how stupid of me!" (All this in his face, for his native tongue is still unintelligible to me.) "That would be impossible. Then how about this?" And then follows another arrangement of saucers for sails, lumps of sugar for steps, and other breakfast accessories illustrating minor details which make it very plain to me that the spot in his mind *now* is lower down the Riva where the fishermen tie their boats to the staircase. This, after all, is really the only spot in Venice worthy the consideration of a great painter on so charming a morning as this.

But I did not want the staircase, and Ingenio saw it. I did, however, want another cup of coffee, and this he brought me.

But where to go, and what to paint! I have learned never to attempt to solve any difficulties in Venice. I fall back on my gondolier.

A section of the Venetian Committee of Finance followed me to my gondola, and a modern Dives added one half of one penny to his wordly store steadying my boat. Ingenio bent to his oar, we glided along the edge of the quay, and I looked back. My gondolier had solved the problem. I would paint the wine shop. My eye had caught the flat quay protected by the marble railing, the glare of the white wall against the deep blue sky, the arching stairway, the soft, filmy outline of the Salute in the distance, and, centring the whole composition, the brilliant-colored awning casting its rich shadow, in which were dotted the groups of wealthy capitalists with the unlimitable bank account of interminable leisure.

An obliging row of houses served as an umbrella and cast a grateful shadow, upon the edge of which I planted my easel. In five minutes more I was working away with as much gusto as if I had planned to paint this identical wine shop weeks before.

The usual Venetian crowd collected and looked over my shoulder. The woman carrying her two copper water-pails slung to a light yoke, and which she had filled at the fountain in the Piazzetta adjoining; the girls stringing beads; the fishermen carrying their nets to the boats moored below; another painter with his trap — etiquette forbids him the privilege of the masses, but all the same I am conscious that he slackens his pace and edges as near as he can, and tiptoes himself for a glance; the tangle-haired children with abbreviated clothing and faces like Raphael's cherubs; the old hags shuffling along in their heelless shoes; the fat priest in his sandals, and the pretty flower-girl in a costume not her own, — all these types are well known to the painter in Venice.

Out on the canal I hear the shouts of the gondoliers and boatmen. My limited knowledge of their language prevents my understanding what the controversy is all about, but all the boatmen on both sides of the water have a voice in it, and I am convinced from the way in which they emphasize some of their expressions that their dialect is punctuated by a very choice variety of profanity.

In the midst of this Babel, which is suddenly increased by the arrival of a number of fruit and fish venders, I hear a strain of music, sung with such a full, free, wholesouled sort of a voice that it drowns all other sounds and instantly catches my ear:—

"Jammo jammo neoppa jammo ja."

It is a Neapolitan song very popular in Venice this summer.

Over the bridge it comes, and in a moment more I catch sight of the singer as he mounts the steps. First his red cap perched on the back of his head, crowning a mass of jet-black hair; then his sunburned face, blue shirt open from the throat to the waist, red sash, and white trousers; and then, as he descends on my side of the bridge, I notice that he is barefooted. A roar of laughter greets him as he halts at the wine shop, and follows him as he makes his way towards the crowd around my easel. Before he reaches me he breaks out again:—

"Jammo jammo neoppa jammo ja.
Funiculi Funiculà Funiculi Funiculà."

Everybody about me welcomes him. The flower-girl gives him a rose, and one of the girls stringing beads a kiss; the old woman a scolding, at which he laughs and makes a grimace, which instantly puts her in a good humor again. As he nears my easel he picks up a child, pinches it, and, when it cries, kisses it and puts it down. Then he plants himself immediately in front of me, completely hiding my view, and cranes his neck trying to see my sketch upside down. He is not impertinent, or rude, or aggressive; he only wants to see what is going on.

I mildly expostulate, and the crowd break out against him in a chorus; and when he cannot be made to understand that he is very much in my way and very much out of his, Ingenio turns up and leads him gently to the rear. Then he sees it all, laughs until the quay rings, pats me on the back, and apologizes like a gentleman.

Before I can reply he dodges into a hallway opposite, hauls out a great seine, spreads it on the marble flagging of the Piazzetta, and falls to mending it with a will, singing at the top of his voice, and stopping every few moments to argue with the girl who is making lace behind her pot of flowers in the balcony over the way, or chaff some gondolier landing at the quay on his left, or send some witticism flying after a passer-by, to the intense delight of the whole community.

This went on for hours, I painting quietly,

and this breezy, happy-hearted, bare-footed, sunburned, rosy-cheeked fisherman keeping the whole place alive and awake. Finally, he gathered up the net just as I finished washing my brushes, stowed it away in his boat near by, waved his hand to me, returned to his house and brought out a table, two chairs, and a bottle of Chianti wine, and, without a moment's hesitation, crossed to where I was packing my sketch-trap, strapped it himself, locked his arm through mine, and led me to his table, his honest, handsome face saying as plain as could be told, "Come, comrade, we have had a hard day's work; now let us have a bottle together." And we did.

I never see a bottle of Chianti but I think of this sunny fisherman, and I never drink one but I pledge him a bumper. I send him my greeting over the sea, and long life to him, and a wife to love him, and plenty of fish, and plenty of Chianti, and one bottle always for me! I owe him my thanks for his hearty laugh, and his song, and his courtesy, and for his share in making this summer's day the pleasantest I spent in Venice.

THE TOP OF A GONDOLA

While I am at breakfast this morning a fleet of lighter boats sweep slowly past my garden and moor to a cluster of piles off the Dogana.

I have been on the lookout for this picturesque flotilla for some time, and Ingenio knows it. Before I have half finished my omelette he arrives off the marble steps, and rounds in his gondola, steadying her against the incoming tide with one hand and waving his congratulations with the other.

One peculiarity of this gentle, loyal soul is the intense personal interest he takes in my affairs. When I am satisfied with my day's work Ingenio is bubbling over with happiness, and hums to himself as he rows along some old song, or rather one line of it. When my sky becomes muddy, or my shadows opaque, and I irritable and disgusted (what painter is not so sometimes?), poor Ingenio pulls aways mute and sad, and comes forward every now and then with an anxious expression upon his face and watches the sketch as if it was a sick child and I the physician upon whom its life depended.

This morning he is as happy over the arrival of these golden-winged boats from beyond the Lido as if he was my man Friday crying a sail! and I his shipwrecked master.

In five minutes we are off, and running under the shadow of the Salute. As it is too hot to work in the sun, moored to a spile on the Canal, I direct Ingenio to the broad landing of the church, hoping to find some spot where I can put up my easel and umbrella and paint the group of lighters in comfort and at my leisure.

I convey this information with my umbrella-staff very much as a Londoner directs and stops a hansom cab with his walking-stick. Ingenio sees the point (of the staff, of course) over the edge of my gondola's awning, darts in among a number of fishing boats, and immediately begins a search in the pavement of the Piazzetta for a crack wide and deep enough in which to anchor my umbrella and still keep sight of the lighters.

This combination proved difficult. There were cracks enough, and views enough; the problem was to utilize them together.

It is true, there was also a long, cool shadow slanting across the marble pavement which would serve as an umbrella, and which for a time was tempting, but sober second thought convinced me that it could not be depended on. It was not the shadow of the great dome of the Salute, but of one of its small towers; and the sun, in his mad climb to the zenith, was fast melting it up.

But if the shadow failed me Ingenio did not, for at that instant he returned from a search after narrow cracks with news of some wide openings. These proved to be half a dozen or more felsi laid up for the summer on the far side of the landing, under which I could crawl and so escape the heat.

The discovery so pleased my faithful gondolier that, without waiting for any instructions from me, he picked up the traps and deposited them in front of a row of great black beetles sprawled out on the pavement, apparently sunning themselves. On closer inspection they proved to be the tops of gondolas used in wet and wintry weather, whose owners, having no immediate use for them, had laid them by for a rainy day like their extra pennies.

I inspected each one in turn, found one larger than the others commanding a capital view of the boats, and crawled in at once.

It made a delightful studio, was just high enough and wide enough, and had two windows on each side, with sliding shutters and sash like a cab's, which proved admirable in managing the light on my canvas.

The result was that I spent the whole day under its shelter, and finally completed my picture, Ingenio bringing me, from one of the fishing boats, some broiled fish and a pot of coffee for luncheon, which I shared with him, he occupying the adjoining felsé, and pushing his cup under mine for me to fill.

When the sun went down and I began

packing up my traps, a number of gondoliers arrived, one of whom, a forbidding-looking fellow with a shock of red hair, informed Ingenio that the felsé belonged to his gondola, and that he demanded eight lira for the use of it. On my replying that he could not earn one quarter of that amount with his *whole* gondola, and that one lira, which I handed him, would be more than a reasonable rent for his stationary sunshade, at best but *half* a gondola, he flew into a great rage, and tossed the lira back to Ingenio. Then finding that I paid no further attention to him and moved off, he collected a crowd of gondoliers, who, uniting their cries to his, jumped into their boats, and followed my own to the water stairs of my lodgings, the whole mob shouting and gesticulating wildly.

There we were met by the porter. He is rather a thin gentleman with a high forehead, and is proverbial for his politeness. As his entire life is spent on the front steps helping people in and out of their gondolas, it is deserved. He performed that service for me, and then turned upon the howling mob.

It was simply delightful to see the way

he handled them. They evidently knew him, and respected either his authority or patronage, — the latter probably.

During the discussion I sought the quiet of the garden, followed by Ingenio, who vented his indignation upon the whole crew, being especially severe upon the gentleman with the auburn locks, whom he described by gestures of infinite disgust.

Before long the porter sought me out, and explained that these gondoliers were a rough set, and that if I valued my peace of mind while in Venice I ought to make some settlement of the affair, and either pay the amount demanded or explain the circumstances to the other gondoliers.

At this juncture an idea occurred to me which I proceeded to put into practice.

I would invite the plaintiff and half a dozen of his confrères into the garden, install the porter as chief justice, and argue the case before him.

This programme was immediately carried out, — the porter acting in the double capacity of interpreter and judge.

The gondolier opened the case. He stated that he had been at work all day, and being too poor to pay some one to watch his felsé had left it unguarded. On his return, in the evening, he had surprised this rich painter as he was leaving it, and who, after occupying it all day, had refused to pay for the privilege, except in a coin of so little value that it was almost an insult to the profession to offer it.

On the cross-examination it was shown that at this season of the year there were several hundred felsi decorating the vacant quays, landings, and piazzas of Venice (there being no back yards in which to store them)`; that a gondola had a summer and a winter top, consequently only one was or could be used at the same time; and that now, in summer time, the felsé I I occupied was about of as much use to the plaintiff as two umbrellas on a rainy day.

It was also shown that the gross earnings of a gondolier and a gondola combined average less than three lira a day, and that there was no instance on record in Venice or elsewhere in which any gondolier had ever collected any large or small amount of money for the use of a felsé for any period of time, long or short.

On the re-direct, the plaintiff wanted the judge and jury to remember that no bargain had been made for the use of the felsé; that accordingly he had a right to charge what he considered would compensate him, especially since there existed no tariff for laid-by felsi; and that, in defiance of his rights of ownership, I had forcibly entered and taken possession.

The effect of this last shot on the jury was very pronounced. They looked at each other wisely, and nodded concurrence.

It was now my turn, and as I was conducting my own case I summed up for the defense.

I asked the jury whether Italy was not now free, and whether Venice was not a city free to her citizens and to the strangers within her gates. I reminded them that the days of Austrian tyranny were days of the past, and that any Italian who would wish to renew them would be a traitor to his country.

In those days a tax was placed upon the people of Venice so severe that the privations it caused were still fresh in their memories.

Now, thanks to a humane government under a wise king, all such onerous burdens had been lifted from the people.

Venice had a free harbor, free canals, free churches, piazzas, and landings.

How came it, then, that this plaintiff, representing so loyal a body of hardworking citizens as the gondoliers, should seek to bring back the days of tyranny and wrong?

The king had said these piazzas were free, and under this ruling I, a stranger, in the peaceful pursuit of my profession, had taken up my position in one of them. I had really occupied the pavement, not the felsé [sensation]; and if its top happened to be over me and so shaded me from the heat of the sun, that circumstance gave the plaintiff no more ground for charging me eight lira for its use than it did the owner of a palace, who happened to own the shady side of the street, and so charged passers-by for the relief it afforded them.

This settled it. The judge decided in favor of the defendant, maintaining that felsi and Venice were free, and that the only charge which could reasonably be made would be against the gondolier for obstructing the painter and annoying him while engaged in the peaceful pursuit of his profession.

Ingenio afterwards reported that the verdict was entirely satisfactory to the jury, and also to the gondolier, who had not seen it in that light before.

When I saw him the next day and handed him again the one lira, he touched his hat and said, " Gracias, signor."

Since this little incident I have been more than ever impressed with the majesty of the law, which somehow or other always seems to protect me in these my wanderings!

BEHIND THE RIALTO

I AM at work painting an old bridge spanning a narrow canal which flows behind the Rialto. It is the sole dependence of a crooked crevice of a street which it helps over and across a sluggish water way and into a small open square facing a church. This bridge also provides shop space for a vender of cheap pottery, whose wares of green and red glisten in the sun, supplying a spot of brilliant color to my composition. I know this church and its quaint interior, and I also know the café next to it, for here Ingenio and I often breakfast. It is an unpretentious place, but the coffee is always good, and sometimes the landlord serves a cutlet sliced quite thin and smothered in an inviting sauce.

This morning I prefer breakfasting in

my gondola, and so send Ingenio for coffee and whatever else he can bring me from a larder rarely overstocked.

If you have never breakfasted in a gondola moored under the windows of an old palace, on its cool side, with your curtains drawn back, the water gurgling about you and reflecting the thousand tints of marble walls, white sails, and blue skies, I commend it to you as an experience which, once enjoyed, you will never forget.

When Ingenio returns with the coffee he brings me a message from the landlord, "that he is cooking a cutlet, and will send it to the bridge." Later on, in looking from between my curtains, I see a pale-faced child, scarce ten years of age, carrying between her outstretched hands a covered dish. I notice, also, that Ingenio helps her carefully down the slippery steps of the landing, relieves her of the cutlet, and when she hesitates and is timid about returning, picks her up gently in his arms, and places her safely on the quay at the entrance of the crevice of a street, through which she disappears waving her hand.

In my experience gondoliers are not in the habit of exhibiting such watchful care over the youth of Venice, and so I ask Ingenio, in our sign language, now quite well understood between us, if the child belongs to him.

The old man smiles sadly, and a faraway look comes into his eyes; then he shakes his head.

The cutlet and sketch finished, the gondola is headed up the canal, and Ingenio and I begin our daily search for good bric-a-brac at poor prices. To-day I want a staff, or boat-hook, similar to one I saw yesterday in the hands of a Venetian gentleman of unlimited leisure, who used it in steadying the gondola of an Englishman of unlimited means, who upon alighting immediately purchased it. It was studded all over with copper coins of various dates and diameters nailed to the wood, a kind of portable savings bank, and was altogether a very curious and interesting exhibit of Venetian life.

Ingenio thinks he knows a gondolier who may still own one. He is to be found at the right-hand landing of the Rialto. So we twist our way in and out of the narrow water ways, and under many bridges, and then through the broad water of the

Grand Canal, spanned by the famous arch. But Ingenio's friend could not be found at the landing, or anywhere else in the vicinity, so we try another bridge lower down, and not finding him there, give up the search in this direction. A shop near the fish-market, another in one of the streets near the Piazzetta, and a fisherman's house above it, were next visited without success. Then Ingenio tells me he thinks he can find a staff near his own home, but a short distance away. Might he turn the gondola into the canal to our left?

He had often before asked me to visit his home. At one time, it was because of a café opposite his house where they made an excellent omelette; again, it was a cabinet-maker, who kept his shop near where he lived, and who had some old engravings in black frames. To-day, it is this much sought for staff.

Until now either want of time or some more interesting excursion had always prevented my consenting, and, when I again refuse, the same sad expression I often see passes over his face, and so, to please him, I nod my head. A few quick strokes bring us to an angle in the canal running behind the Rialto, and quite near where I had breakfasted in the morning.

A pleasant-faced woman, prematurely old, comes down a flight of steps built under a culvert-shaped arch, and holds the boat to the lower step. It is Ingenio's wife. I follow her under the arch, up a tottering flight of steps, and into a small, scrupulously clean room with high ceiling. It is their living room, and, like all Venetian kitchens, has its fire-place built out from the wall, while on either side of the raised hearth, two small windows, about one foot square, look out on the canal. The shelf over the hearth, and the wall above it, shine with well-polished brass and copper pans. White curtains soften the glare of the sunlight. Some pictures of the Holy Mother, a cheap crucifix, and a few articles of furniture complete the interior. Ingenio enters, having moored the gondola, gives me the best chair, draws the curtains that I may see the view of the Grand Canal and the Rialto, officiates as sign-interpreter between me and his wife, and then disappears into an adjoining room, leaving the door ajar. The good wife rises quickly and closes it behind him.

As she regains her seat she says something to me in Italian which I do not understand.

In a moment more the door reopens and Ingenio enters, carrying in his arms a pale, hollow-cheeked child, about ten years of age, who looks at me wonderingly with her great round eyes. One hand is wound around her father's neck, her thin fingers lost in his bushy gray beard. The other holds a short crutch. I shall never forget the tender way with which the old man placed her on a low stool at his side, caressing her hair, holding fast her hand, and talking to her in a low undertone in his soft Italian; nor the tremor in his voice when he leaned over to me and said, pointing to his crippled daughter: —

"This one belongs to me."

It was all the child he had, poor fellow. She filled his heart full with her bright face and loving ways, and although she was his greatest sorrow, he was proud of her, and proud that I had seen her. Several years ago she had fallen from one of the bridges, struck a passing boat, and broken her thigh. Since then she had lived in these two rooms.

I understood now why he lifted ashore so tenderly my little waitress with the cutlet.

When I regained my gondola I reminded Ingenio of the object of our search. Was the man at home? Had he seen the staff? Would he bring it to the boat? He hung his head, and did not move.

Then it all came out. There was no man with a gondola staff. There had been no cabinet-maker next door, with rare old engravings in black frames, nor any cafés with toothsome omelettes.

It was Giulietta he wanted me to see.

Patient, loyal, gentle, old gondolier! With me you will forever be a part of sunny skies, old palaces, and the silver shimmer of the Lido, the bright sails of red and gold, the cool of dim, incense-laden churches, and crooked canals under quaint bridges.

Even now I hear your warning cry as you round the sharp corners of the canals. But I love best to remember you with that pale-faced child in your arms.

UP A BELFRY IN BAVARIA

I AM aware that this is rather an indefinite belfry, for Bavaria covers a wide territory, and belfries are by no means rare; but, nevertheless, this is as near as any one will ever get to the exact locality of this particular belfry from any information which I will furnish, and there are good reasons for my reticence.

This belfry caps the quaint tower of a curious old Franciscan monastery. It is built of red sandstone, seamed and scarred by the weathers of many centuries, and barnacled all over with gray lichen and green moss. It carries within its open arches the remnant of a chime of bells which are never rung, and overlooks a clock which ran down some hundred years ago, and has never been wound up since. Backed up against the wall of this monastery is a small church or chapel. Adjoining the church is a cloister, surrounded by a high wall, on one side of which is an open gate or archway, the whole surmounted by a high peaked roof.

I had walked up from the lower part of the town, where some quaint houses leaning over a narrow canal, reminding one of two old crones gossiping across a street, had tempted me to paint them, and catching sight of this gate, I loitered in aimlessly. Under the groined arches of the cloister were sheltered idle carts and wagons. From the sculptured tombs in the pavement many restless feet had wellnigh effaced all traces of the graven names of the holy saints who lay buried beneath. It was easy to see that modern Protestantism had no respect for the traditions of the Holy Church.

Crossing the cloister with its vistas of open squares and small culvert-shaped arches running under rickety houses, I passed a group of heavy columns supporting a low roof, the whole forming a vaulted room. A grated window at one end cast a dim light over an old woman washing. She gazed at me solemnly, and pointed to a door in the wall. Thinking that this was another way out, I turned the knob, and found myself in the refectory of the monastery and confronted by a kindly-faced old friar and a strong smell of cookery. It was some time before I could make him understand how I came there and by what mistake, for my knowledge of German is only that of a traveler. My sketch-book, however, settled it. He turned over the leaves slowly, recognized a pencil memorandum of the gate, took my hat from my hand, hung it on one of a row of wooden pegs, and motioning me to a seat, dipped a long perforated iron ladle into a steaming caldron, dished out some boiled potatoes and shreds of meat, and placed them on a plate before me. I thanked him and ate my rations like a friar.

Then I followed him through the wide, bare, white-washed rooms of the ground floor, and into the small church, and such a shabby old church, too! Cheap silvered candlesticks, cheaper cotton lace on the altar-cloth, paper flowers in china vases, ugly modern lamps, German lithographs edged with gilt paper supplying the places of Raphaels and Correggios, and offering candles, none of which were burning, fastened to iron spikes, from which flowed streams of tallow telling of former prayers. All indicated bitter poverty.

Even the wrinkled old friar seemed a part of the place, — sad, hollow-eyed, and barefooted, his waist bound with a cord from which hung a wooden cross, and he himself as much a tear-stained relic of the past as the walls over which the damp of ages had trickled. Poor old fellow! I can see him now looking at me wistfully and standing patiently as I examined all he showed me.

Finally he said to me, "English?" "No," I replied, "American." He dropped the iron hoop which held his keys, and the tears started to his eyes. "American, my son?" Then he took my hand and by many signs and gestures made me understand that my country was the future home of his church; that Bavaria in the dim past had seen the grandeur and splendor of the monastery, which had once been heaped full of riches, and had once been proud of its power and prestige, but now she had turned her back upon it and had left it to decay. As he spoke he picked up a small copper censer, poured the ashes out in the palm of his hand, and sifted them slowly on the floor.

I encouraged him to talk, and examined with him the altar-screen faced with a square of some cheap modern fabric, and asked him what it was like in the olden times? "Velvet and satin, my son, and embroidery of gold and silver; and the lamps all solid gold; the walls were covered with paintings, the steps of the altar with fine carpets; and the Archbishop, to whom the king kneeled, was clothed in lace and scarlet."

By this time we had circled the small church and reached the door, but I was not satisfied. I led him back to the altar and pointed out the different objects. Where *now* was the old lace? Was it stored away somewhere and only shown to travelers? He shook his head and spread his fingers as if it had slipped through them years before. Candlesticks? Lamps? Censers? Still the same mournful shake.

All gone. About the silks and velvets and embroideries that covered the face of the altar; where now were they? He simply cast his eyes upward. But this was a new piece but a few years old; what was done with the old one? A gleam of intelligence shot across his wrinkled old face, and one long, thin finger rested on his forehead. He looked at me searchingly from under his bushy gray eyebrows, tapped me on the shoulder, and led the way back through the bare wide rooms and into the seething refectory, and up to a row of hooks from which hung keys of all shapes and sizes. He looked them over carefully, and took down a great hoop linking three keys together, lighted a lantern, and I followed him into the vault-shaped room, past the old woman, who bowed and crossed herself, through an open court, from which I saw the belfry with the silent chimes, and up to a door in its tower heavily grated with iron.

The first key started its rusty bolts, then we groped our way up a mouldy stone staircase, the friar going ahead feeling his way and holding the lantern for me until we reached the landing of the first story, which I noticed was level with the roof of the monastery. The daylight struggling in through diamond-shaped panes of glass begrimed with dirt and cobwebs revealed another door. I looked through its gratings but saw nothing but an empty room. The old friar pressed his shrunken cheek against the bars, gave a pleased chuckle, unlocked them, and pointed to a pile of six wooden altar screens leaning against the wall and half buried in dust. My heart sank within me.

Not seeing my chagrin he stooped over and threw down the first screen. A cloud of dust arose nearly suffocating me. It proved to be a worm-eaten frame covered with mouldy canvas. The second, the same; the third, mere shreds of worsted, with patches of tinsel lace bearing the figure of the cross embroidered in faded green. The fourth of silk, threadbare and stained with the droppings of many candles. As the dust cleared away from each screen the old fellow would look anxiously in my face for approval. The fifth — to tell you the truth, the fifth took my breath away. It was an old gold-colored corded silk, as heavy as canvas, and covered with an exquisite embroidery in silk and silver without a break or flaw. The canvas backing had protected it from the damp, and the sixth screen against the wall had saved it in a measure from the grime of years.

I broke all the blades of my knife cutting this precious relic of the seventeenth century from its frame, the good friar on his knees meanwhile holding one end taut so that I could run my knife close to the rusted tacks.

His enthusiasm was delightful as he read my face, for the discovery was evidently as much of a surprise to him as to me. "Now I would believe the truth of all the stories of the magnificence of the olden times." And then he lifted it tenderly and carried it as carefully down the treacherous staircase as if it had been blessed by the Pope, and spread it on the grass in the sunlight.

I sat down upon the tomb of an old saint and feasted my eyes.

It was Italian, without doubt, worked in twisted silk and silver in a design of leaves and flowers, the whole in delicate tones of pale yellows, pinks, and turquoise blue. Soiled and stained, of course, but that did not trouble me. I knew a little Frenchwoman near St. Cloud who could take half a loaf of fresh bread and with it work a charm upon its old gold background.

Then I tried a charm of my own with some new gold upon the palm of my old friar. To my surprise he refused it. "No, take it to America. They would appreciate it there. It was nothing here, — all dead, all ashes, all forgotten." Well, then, for the poor? Yes, he would take it for the poor. There were plenty of them always. He would give the money to the bishop for the poor.

As he pressed my hand at the gate his eyes filled, and pointing to the monastery he said slowly, "Never here, my son. In America."

It was not until I reached my lodgings with my prize that I thought of the sixth screen, which in my great joy I had neglected to turn down. What could that have been?

This question I am not yet able to answer, and until I am I shall not tell anybody where in Bavaria is my belfry.

www.ingramcontent.com/pod-product-compliance
Lightning Source LLC
Chambersburg PA
CBHW020110170426
43199CB00009B/476